To Fly Like a Bird	2
Aviation Pioneers	6
Aerobatics	10
Women Aviators	12
War-birds	14
Start of Air Travel	16
Trailblazers	18
Spirit of St. Louis	22
Southern Cross	24
Jean Batten	26
Small Beginnings	28
Glossary	30

To Fly Like a Bird

For thousands of years, people have dreamed of flying. From time to time, daring people attached feathers to their arms and jumped off high places, flapping their "wings" furiously. Their attempts were unsuccessful.

Sir George Cayley made the first breakthrough in human flight. He realized that trying to copy the flapping wings of a bird was probably a waste of time. Instead, he studied the outstretched wings of soaring birds, then designed and built gliders with fixed wings.

In 1849, Sir George rolled one of his "aircraft" down a slope with a ten-year-old boy on board as the pilot. The boy was able to glide the aircraft for several metres, before landing it safely.

3

It was not until 1903, at a place called Kitty Hawk, in North Carolina, U.S.A., that the first powered flight was made. It wasn't a long flight, only about 300 paces for a person, but it was the beginning. The centuries when people could only dream of flying had finally come to an end.

One early aviator was attacked by an eagle that was probably startled by this intruder in its flight path.

The glider (above) provided the basic framework for one of the first powered "flying machines" (below).

Aviation Pioneers

The first truly successful aircraft were built by pioneers working on opposite sides of the world. The *Wright brothers* in the United States of America, and *Richard Pearse* in New Zealand, both built and flew aircraft at about the same time.

Wilbur and Orville Wright built their own lightweight petrol engine to power the two propellers that were fitted to an aircraft named the *Flyer*. Tests were carried out on the *Flyer* over sand dunes in Kitty Hawk, North Carolina. The area was chosen because of its steady wind and, more importantly, because the sand would provide a soft landing if things went wrong!

Test flights completed, the Wright brothers' *Flyer* takes to the air.

Pioneering aviator – Richard Pearse

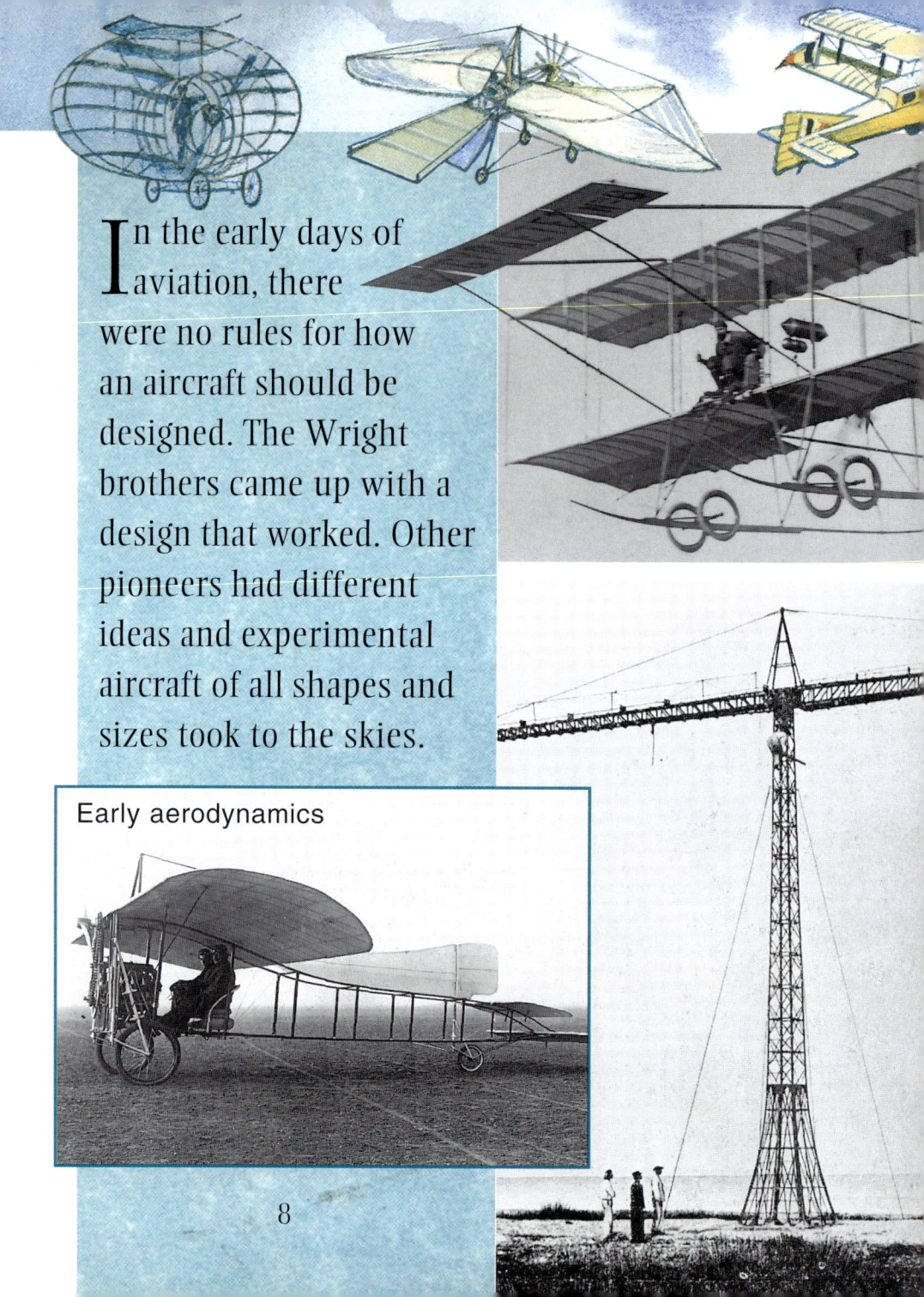

In the early days of aviation, there were no rules for how an aircraft should be designed. The Wright brothers came up with a design that worked. Other pioneers had different ideas and experimental aircraft of all shapes and sizes took to the skies.

Early aerodynamics

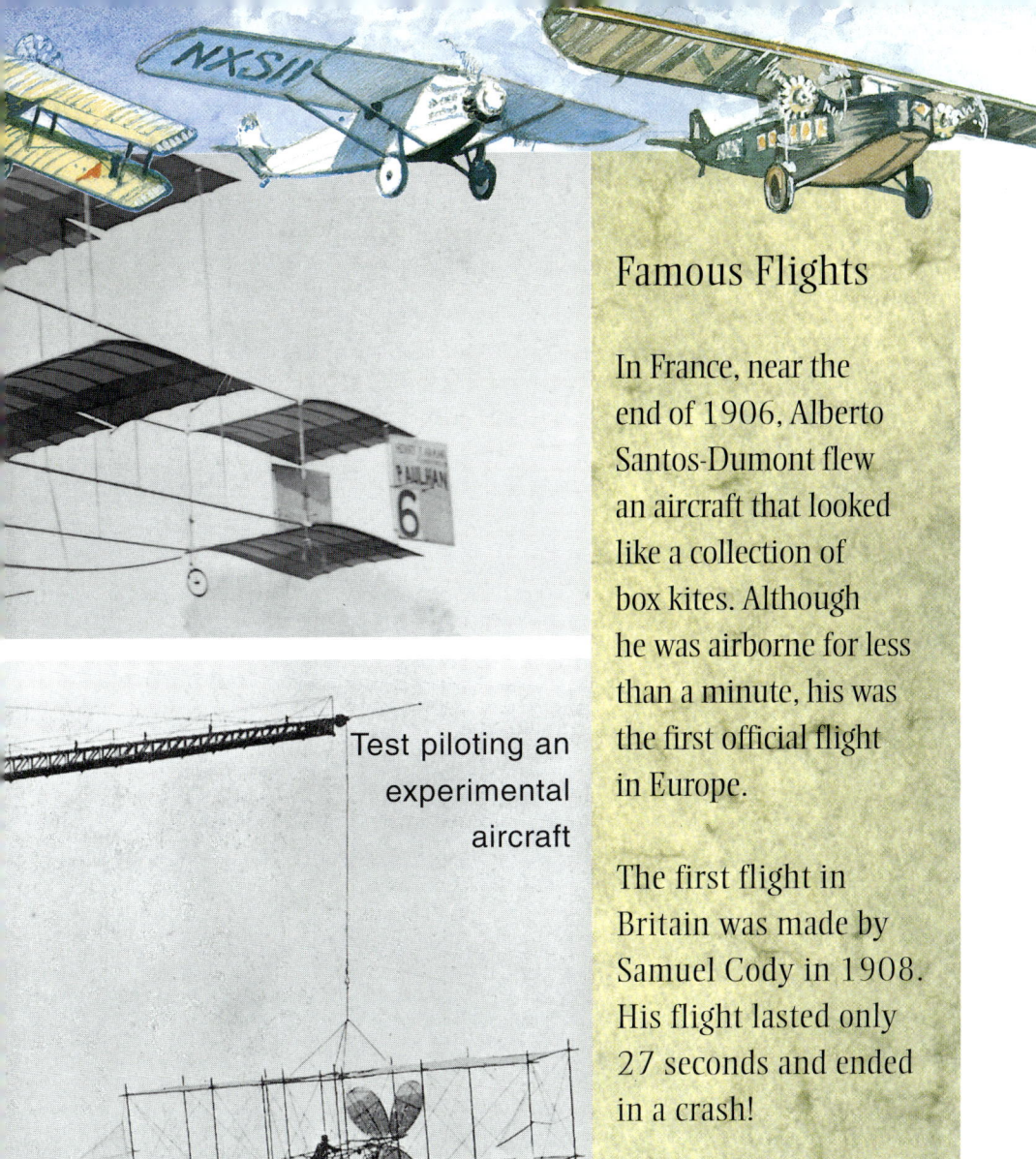

Test piloting an experimental aircraft

Famous Flights

In France, near the end of 1906, Alberto Santos-Dumont flew an aircraft that looked like a collection of box kites. Although he was airborne for less than a minute, his was the first official flight in Europe.

The first flight in Britain was made by Samuel Cody in 1908. His flight lasted only 27 seconds and ended in a crash!

Aerobatics

In 1908, Wilbur Wright took a new aeroplane to Europe. It could turn, circle, and fly in a figure eight. He was in the air for a lengthy 2 hours and 20 seconds. Everyone was astonished.

Before long, air shows and air races became great public attractions. These events helped to improve aircraft design and pilot skills. To please the crowds, pilots performed dangerous aerobatics. Spectacular flyers became popular heroes.

Wilbur Wright demonstrates the latest in aviation technology.

Women Aviators

When aviation first began, many people believed that flying was a male "sport". Many women thought otherwise. In March, 1910, a French woman, *Raymonde de Laroche*, became the world's first woman pilot. She was soon followed by pioneering aviator, *Harriet Quimby*, of the United States.

Helene Dutrieu

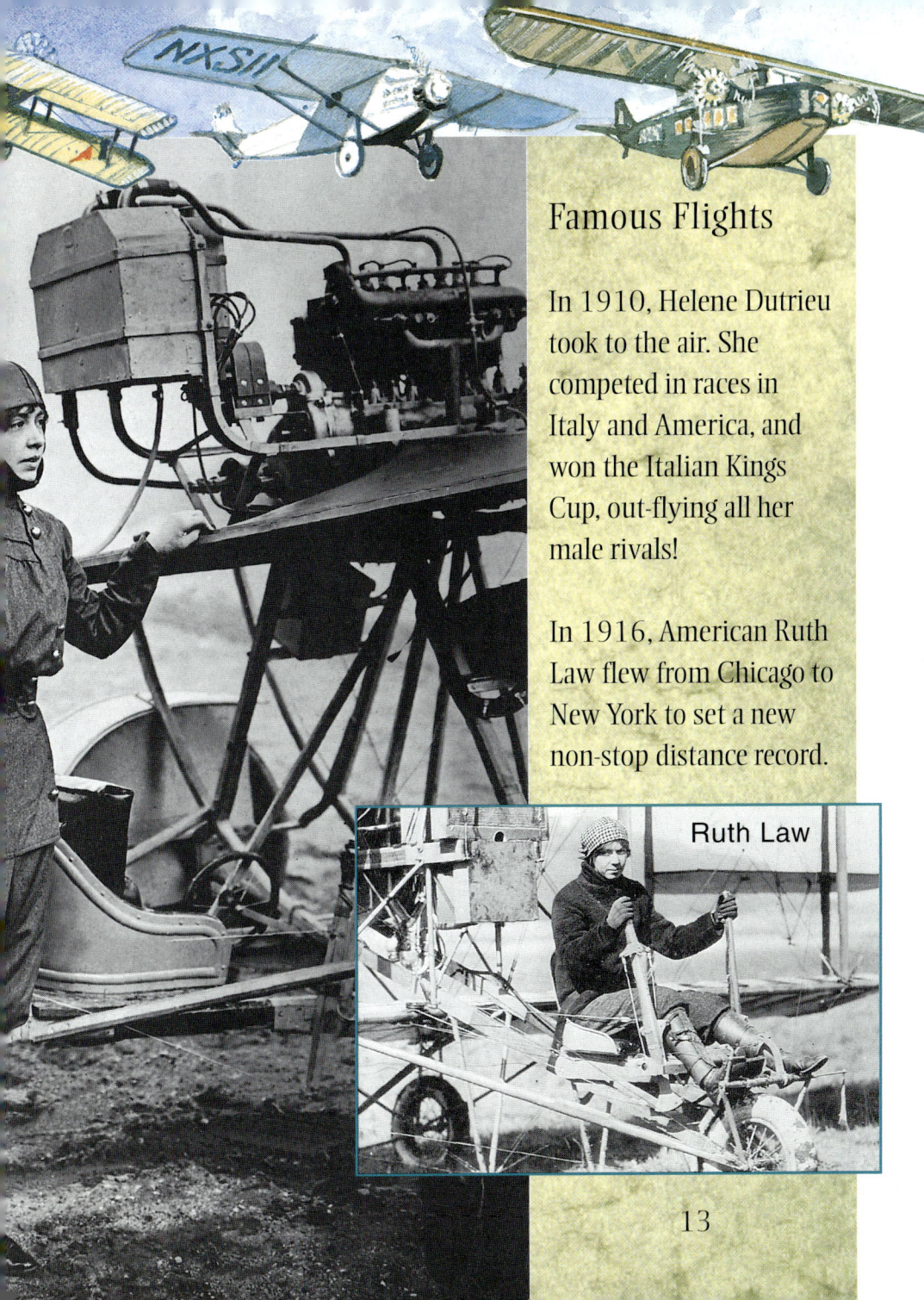

Famous Flights

In 1910, Helene Dutrieu took to the air. She competed in races in Italy and America, and won the Italian Kings Cup, out-flying all her male rivals!

In 1916, American Ruth Law flew from Chicago to New York to set a new non-stop distance record.

Ruth Law

War-birds

Just as the world began to consider flying as a useful form of transportation, the First World War broke out in Europe. The plane became a weapon of war.

World-famous air ace Baron Manfred von Richthofen was known as the Red Baron because his triplane was painted bright red.

Many pilots made a name for themselves during the war, when daring dogfights were fought in the skies.

Start of Air Travel

When peace returned in 1918, there were many trained pilots and unwanted aircraft. Old warplanes were often converted to carry passengers. The pilots, fitted with goggles and flying helmets, sat in open cockpits. Passengers were provided with helmets, goggles, gloves, blankets, and hot-water bottles for their cold journey! This was the start of commercial air travel and airlines.

Breakdowns and mishaps were frequent. Bad weather could cause many delays and dangers. At first, few people were willing to fly. They looked upon aviators as exciting figures, but weren't convinced that flying was really safe.

Trailblazers

When the war ended, aircraft builders concentrated on producing planes for the peacetime adventures of exploring pilots, who became known as Trailblazers. The challenge to fly long distances and to cross the sea by air was enticing.

Many heroic pilots took off in their frail little aircraft and flew into the unknown. Some set records for others to follow and break. Others were defeated by violent storms. Crashes were common, and many early aviators lost their lives.

Famous Flights

In 1909, Louis Bleriot, flew across the English Channel. He just managed to clear the cliffs of Dover before landing awkwardly in a field and breaking the aircraft's propeller.

In 1913, Roland Garros flew across the Mediterranean Sea from France to North Africa. He reached North Africa with a damaged motor and only four litres of fuel to spare.

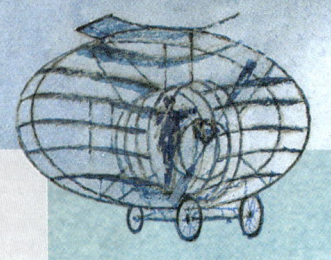  

Each new flight established an air route and enabled the speedy delivery of mail. Carrying the mail was a very important part of flying in the early years. A bag of mail was often transported in an explorer's aircraft.

After *Alcock and Brown* crossed the Atlantic and crash-landed in Ireland, they handed over a sack of letters. Charles Lindbergh, one of aviation's greatest heroes, began his career as an airmail pilot.

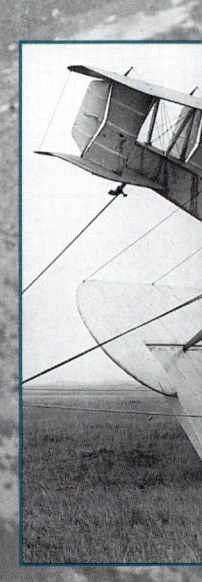

Famous Flights

Cailbraith Rodgers made the first flight across the United States, from New York to California, in 1911. He landed or crashed his aeroplane about 70 times! The journey took 84 days, but the actual flying time was only 3 days, 10 hours, and 24 minutes.

Aviators Alcock and Brown crossed the Atlantic in 1919. Their journey in a converted bomber ended with a spectacular crash-landing in an Irish bog!

Spirit of St. Louis

In 1927, Charles Lindbergh flew solo across the Atlantic from New York to Paris in a plane called the *Spirit of St. Louis*. It was early aviation's most famous flight.

From where he sat in the tiny cabin, the only way Lindbergh could see where he was going was to look through a periscope. He was in the air for an exhausting 33 hours. It was getting dark as he approached Paris, but the light from hundreds of beacons guided him overland and safely into the city.

Lindbergh took only five sandwiches and a canteen of water for the journey. His greatest fear on the long trip was of falling asleep, so he didn't eat the sandwiches in the hope that hunger would keep him awake!

Southern Cross

The largest of all the oceans, the Pacific, was yet to be flown. Most people believed the Pacific was too wide to be crossed by air. An Australian, Charles Kingsford Smith, set out to prove them wrong.

On May 31, 1928, Kingsford Smith took off from San Francisco in a plane called the *Southern Cross*, and headed out over the Pacific. His partner, Charles Ulm, and two crew members flew with him.

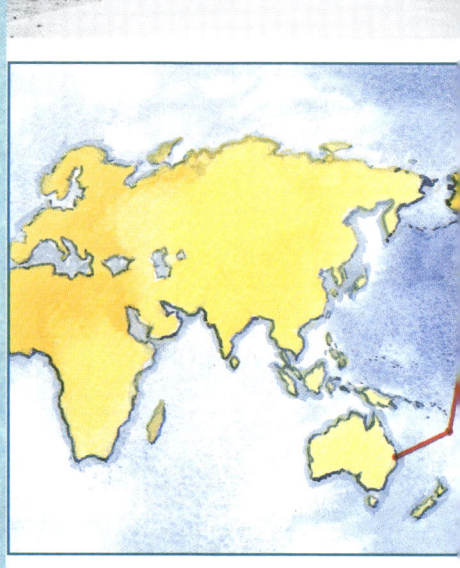

The stretch to Hawaii had been flown before, but nobody had ever flown across the ocean to Fiji. The greatest problem was finding such a tiny speck of an island in such a huge expanse of sea. The aviators succeeded and arrived in Brisbane, Australia, on June 10.

The aviators then made the first-ever crossing of the stormy Tasman Sea to New Zealand. Later, they flew from Australia to London, then on to San Francisco, completing a circuit of the world.

Jean Batten

In 1934, this young New Zealand-born woman flew solo from England to Australia and back again, becoming the first woman to make the two-way trip. Hampered by tropical storms and strong head-winds, her return flight took 17 days, 15 hours, and 15 minutes. When she arrived, her hands were a mass of blisters and sores.

Jean Batten went on to make many epic flights. Throughout her career, she had numerous close encounters with disaster. She flew through fierce storms, survived engine failure and forced landings, navigated without a radio or a compass, and even crash-landed in a swamp!

Famous Flights

In 1935, Jean Batten made the fastest crossing of the South Atlantic Ocean, from Africa to Brazil. She was the first woman to fly this route.

In 1936, Batten became the first person to fly direct from England to New Zealand. It was her most famous flight. She was also the first woman to fly the Tasman Sea.

Small Beginnings

By 1937, air travel was beginning to catch on and most people knew about aeroplanes. Many thought of them as noisy, but fascinating, machines. Often, great crowds turned out to watch daring stunts at air shows, or to welcome flyers arriving from far-away lands. From these small beginnings, a world-wide airline industry has grown. It has all happened in a very short, but very exciting, time in history.

In 1937, the world's most modern airport was Croydon, in London. It had a terminal building and a control tower, but the runway was a grass strip that was mowed twice a year using a horse-drawn mowing machine.

29

Glossary

Alcock and Brown – the pioneering British aviators were knighted by King George V for their successful world-first non-stop transatlantic flight in June, 1919.

Cayley, Sir George – lived in England during the nineteenth century. He is regarded as the "father" of aviation.

de Laroche, Raymonde – a french baroness, born in 1886, dared enter what had been strictly male territory, becoming the first woman to hold a pilot's licence.

Pearse, Richard – lived on a farm in the South Island of New Zealand. His successful pioneering experiments with flying were not fully recognized until after his death.

Quimby, Harriet – had a short, but successful, flying career. She flew across Mexico and also across the English Channel. She was killed in a flying accident in 1917.

Wright brothers, Orville and Wilbur – were bicycle makers in Dayton, Ohio. They experimented with kites and gliders before building their first powered flying machine.

Taking to the Air

ISBN 13: 978-0-79-011657-0
ISBN 10: 79-011657-X

 **Kingscourt**

Published by:
McGraw-Hill Education
Shoppenhangers Road, Maidenhead, Berkshire, England, SL6 2QL
Telephone: 44 (0) 1628 502730
Fax: 44 (0) 1628 635895
Website: www.kingscourt.co.uk
Website: www.mcgraw-hill.co.uk

Written by **David Lowe**
Illustrated by **Bryan Pollard**
Edited by **Lynette Evans**
Designed by **Nicola Evans**
Cover designed by **Warren Sly** and **Nicola Evans**
Photographic Research by **Sarah Irvine**

Photography by Culver Pictures: (p.8; Ruth Law, p.13; passenger plane, pp. 20-21; p.22); **Fotopacific:** (Orville Wright, 1903, p.5; p.15; p.23); **Photobank Image Library:** Hulton Getty collection (pp. 8-11; the Wright glider, 1902, p.5; Helene Dutrieu, pp. 12-13; pp. 18-19; crash landing, pp. 20-21; pp. 24-25; Jean Batten at croydon, pp. 26-27; pp. 28-29); **Qantas Airways Limited:** (pp. 16-17); **U.S. Postal Service:** (postage stamp, p.12); **Walsh Memorial Library/MOTAT:** (p.7; Jean Batten, p.27)

Original Edition © 1997 Shortland Publications
English Reprint Edition © 2009 McGraw Hill Publishing Company

All rights reserved. No part of this publication may be reproduced or tranmitted in any form or by any means, electronic or mechanical, including photocopying, recording, or any information storage and retrieval system, without written permission from the publisher.

Printed in Hong Kong through Colorcraft Ltd.

From the Author

When my father was born, no one had ever flown in a powered flying machine. When I was born, the first jet aircraft were being tested. When my son was born, people were preparing to go to the moon!

When I was a boy, the sky over our family home was busy with aeroplanes every day. I have always had an interest in the history of flight. I enjoy watching aircraft take off and land, and I quite like flying. But I don't think I would like to fly in some of the aircraft that are in this book!

David Lowe